THE LITTLE BOOK OF
TRUMP

Published by Orange Hippo!
20 Mortimer Street
London W1T 3JW

ISBN 978-1-91161-031-1

Editorial: Stella Caldwell, Victoria Godden
Project Manager: Russell Porter
Design: Tony Seddon
Production: Jessica Arvidsson

A CIP catalogue for this book is available from the British Library

Printed in Dubai

10 9 8 7 6 5 4 3 2 1

Jacket cover photograph: Jeff J Mitchell/Getty Images

THE LITTLE BOOK OF

TRUMP

IN HIS OWN WORDS

CONTENTS

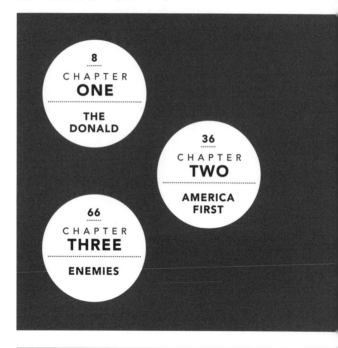

INTRODUCTION

Summing up the whirlwind life and times of Donald J. Trump is a challenge in itself, but he is a man who has always said and done exactly what he wants – because he can.

As a billionaire businessman, fast-living celebrity and now the most powerful man on Earth, Trump is someone that people take notice of – even when his utterances bear little or no resemblance to reality. And he is a man who is never short of a word or two, whether he's dishing out advice in his best-selling business books, playing to his adoring fan base at huge rallies, or blasting his enemies in furious late-night tweets.

Donald Trump has been labelled the "king of social media" and he thrives on the oxygen that outraged newspaper headlines and TV coverage give him. His first-ever tweet, in May 2009, was tame by anyone's standards – "Be sure to tune in and watch Donald Trump on Late Night with David Letterman as he presents the Top Ten List tonight!" But since then, his tweets have become ever wilder and more frequent. His Twitter account has amassed 65.2 million followers, and in September 2019 alone, the President tweeted a record 800 times. In addition, his rally speeches have become longer (and angrier), and his hours spent talking on camera have risen sharply too.

Given that extraordinary output, it's little wonder it can be hard to keep up with the views of the Donald. But whether you love him or loathe him – and he is a man who *definitely* divides opinion – taking stock of just some of the things he has said over the past three decades is a fascinating / illuminating / entertaining / terrifying (delete as appropriate) exercise!

CHAPTER
ONE

THE DONALD

"

I like thinking big. I always have. To me it's very simple: if you're going to be thinking anyway, you might as well think big. Most people think small, because most people are afraid of success, afraid of making decisions, afraid of winning. And that gives people like me a great advantage.

"

Trump: The Art of the Deal, *1987*

"

The final key to the way I promote is bravado. I play to people's fantasies. People may not always think big themselves, but they can still get very excited by those who do. That's why a little hyperbole never hurts. People want to believe that something is the biggest and the greatest and the most spectacular. I call it truthful hyperbole. It's an innocent form of exaggeration – and a very effective form of promotion.

"

Trump: The Art of the Deal, *1987*

66

You know, it really doesn't matter what [the media] write, as long as you've got a young and beautiful piece of ass.

99

Esquire, *1991*

66

To be blunt, people would vote for me. They just would. Why? Maybe because I'm so good looking. **99**

New York Times, *19 September 1999*

66

I think Viagra is wonderful if you need it, if you have medical issues… I've just never needed it. Frankly, I wouldn't mind if there were an anti-Viagra, something with the opposite effect. I'm not bragging. I'm just lucky. I don't need it.

99

Playboy, *October 2004*

" No animals have been harmed in the creation of my hairstyle. **"**

Trump: How to Get Rich, *2004*

66

Oftentimes when I was sleeping with one of the top women in the world, I would say to myself, thinking about me as a boy from Queens, 'Can you believe what I am getting?'

99

Think Big: Make it Happen in Business and in Life, *2008*

66

Part of the beauty of me is that
I am very rich.

99

Good Morning America,
ABC, March 2011

66

My fingers are long and beautiful,
as, it has been well documented,
are various other parts of
my body.

99

Page Six, *2011*

66

My motto is: Always get even.
When somebody screws you,
screw them back in spades. **99**

Think Big and Kick Ass in Business, *2012*

66

As everybody knows, but
the haters & losers refuse to
acknowledge, I do not wear a
'wig.' My hair may not be
perfect but it's mine.

99

Twitter, 24 April 2013

66

I'm actually a nice person. I try very hard to be a nice person. **99**

Fox News, September 2014

66

Money was never a big motivation
for me, except as a way to keep
score. The real excitement is
playing the game!

99

Twitter, 14 September 2014

66

I will be the greatest jobs president
that God ever created.

99

Candidacy announcement speech,
16 June 2015

66

I could stand in the middle of Fifth Avenue and shoot somebody, and I wouldn't lose any voters, okay? It's, like, incredible.

99

Iowa rally, 23 January 2016

66

Look at those hands. Are they small hands? And [Republican rival Marco Rubio] referred to my hands: 'If they're small, something else must be small.' I guarantee you there's no problem. I guarantee.

99

Fox News debate, 3 March 2016

"

That makes me smart.

"

Responding to Hillary Clinton's suggestion that he pays no federal income tax, 26 September 2016

We are going to have an unbelievable, perhaps record-setting turnout for the inauguration, and there will be plenty of movie and entertainment stars. All the dress shops are sold out in Washington. It's hard to find a great dress for this inauguration.

New York Times, *January 2017*

66

I loved my previous life. I had so many things going. This is more work than in my previous life. I thought it would be easier.

99

Reuters, 27 April 2017

No one has better respect
for intelligence than
Donald Trump.

Press conference, 8 November 2017

"

Actually, throughout my life, my two greatest assets have been mental stability and being, like, really smart. Crooked Hillary Clinton also played these cards very hard and, as everyone knows, went down in flames. I went from VERY successful businessman, to top TV Star... to President of the United States (on my first try). I think that would qualify as not smart, but genius... and a very stable genius at that!

"

Twitter, 6 January 2018

66

I really believe I'd run in there, even if I didn't have a weapon.

99

Commenting on the Parkland High School mass shooting, 27 February 2018

"

Lowest-rated Oscars in HISTORY.
Problem is, we don't have Stars
anymore – except your President
(just kidding, of course)!

"

Twitter, 6 March 2018

When I came into office people thought we were going into nuclear war, OK, and now they're saying 'wow'… I'd give myself an A+.

Fox News, 27 April 2018

66

After having written many best-selling books, and somewhat priding myself on my ability to write, it should be noted that the Fake News constantly likes to pore over my tweets looking for a mistake. I capitalize certain words only for emphasis, not b/c they should be capitalized!

99

Twitter, 4 July 2018

66

Nobody has ever done so
much in the first two years of a
presidency as this administration.
Nobody. Nobody.

99

Mississippi speech, 26 November 2018

CHAPTER
TWO

AMERICA FIRST

66

I was tired, and I think a lot
of other people are tired of
watching other people ripping
off the United States. This is a
great country. They laugh at us.
Behind our backs, they laugh
at us because of our
own stupidity.

99

Speaking to Larry King, CNN, 1987

66

Probably not. But I do get tired of seeing the country get ripped off.

99

On being asked if he would ever run for President, The Oprah Winfrey Show, *April 1988*

"

The US cannot allow EBOLA-infected people back.
People that go to far-away places to help out are great – but must suffer the consequences!

"

Twitter, 2 August 2014

66

Citizenship is not a gift we can afford to keep giving away.

99

Crippled America, *2015*

"

The idea of American Greatness, of our country as the leader of the free and unfree world, has vanished… I couldn't stand to see what was happening to our great country. This mess calls for leadership in the worst way.

"

Crippled America, *2015*

> **❝**
> I think the big problem this country has is being politically correct. I've been challenged by so many people and I don't, frankly, have time for total political correctness. **❞**

Fox News debate, 8 June 2015

66

I will build a great wall – and nobody builds walls better than me, believe me – and I'll build them very inexpensively. I will build a great, great wall on our southern border and I will make Mexico pay for that wall. Mark my words.

99

*Candidacy announcement speech,
16 June 2015*

Our country is in serious trouble. We don't have victories anymore. We used to have victories, but we don't have them. When was the last time anybody saw us beating, let's say, China in a trade deal? They kill us. I beat China all the time. All the time.

Candidacy announcement speech,
16 June 2015

"

The right of the people to keep
and bear arms shall not be
infringed upon. Period.

"

Campaign policy speech,
September 2015

66

Gun and magazine bans are a total failure. That's been proven every time it's been tried... The government has no business dictating what types of firearms good, honest people are allowed to own.

99

Campaign leaflet, 2015

"

I was down there, and I watched our police and our firemen, down on 7-Eleven, down at the World Trade Center, right after it came down.

"

Confusing a convenience store with 9/11, campaign rally, 19 April 2016

66

SEE YOU IN COURT, THE
SECURITY OF OUR NATION IS
AT STAKE!

99

*After a halt on an executive order
restricting travel to the US from seven
Muslim-majority countries was upheld,
Twitter, 9 February 2017*

66

Mothers and children trapped in poverty in our inner cities; rusted-out factories scattered like tombstones across the landscape of our nation; an education system flush with cash but which leaves our young and beautiful students deprived of knowledge; and the crime and gangs and drugs that have stolen too many lives and robbed our country of so much unrealized potential. This American carnage stops right here and stops right now.

99

Inaugural address, 20 January 2017

"

From this day forward, it's going to be only America first, America first. Every decision on trade, on taxes, on immigration, on foreign affairs will be made to benefit American workers and American families.

"

Inaugural address, 20 January 2017

66

Terrible! Just found out that
Obama had my 'wires tapped'
in Trump Tower just before the
victory. Nothing found. This is
McCarthyism!

99

Twitter, 4 March 2017

"

Well, I do think there's blame –
yes, there's blame on both sides.
You look at – you look at both
sides. I think there's blame on
both sides.

"

*On the violence that erupted at a
white nationalist rally in Charlottesville,
Virginia, 12 August 2017*

66

Courageous Patriots have fought and died for our great American Flag – we MUST honor and respect it! MAKE AMERICA GREAT AGAIN!

99

Twitter, 24 September 2017

"

The American public is fed up with the disrespect the NFL is paying to our Country, our Flag and our National Anthem. Weak and out of control!

"

Twitter, 28 November 2017

Throughout our history, the American people have always been the true source of American greatness. Our people have promoted our culture and promoted our values. Americans have fought and sacrificed on the battlefields all over the world. We have liberated captive nations, transformed former enemies into the best of friends, and lifted entire regions of the planet from poverty to prosperity...

…Our leaders drifted from American principles. They lost sight of America's destiny. And they lost their belief in American greatness. As a result, our citizens lost something as well. The people lost confidence in their government and, eventually, even lost confidence in their future. But last year, all of that began to change. The American people rejected the failures of the past.

99

*Security strategy speech,
18 December 2017*

66

Why are we having all these
people from shithole countries
come here?

99

*Meeting about protections for
immigrants, 11 January 2018*

The United States has an $800 Billion Dollar Yearly Trade Deficit because of our 'very stupid' trade deals and policies. Our jobs and wealth are being given to other countries that have taken advantage of us for years. They laugh at what fools our leaders have been. No more!

Twitter, 3 March 2018

66

You go to the hospital. You have a broken arm. You come out, you are a drug addict with this crap. **99**

Referencing the opioid crisis,
Nashville speech, 29 May 2018

This is a tough hurricane...
One of the wettest we've ever
seen from the standpoint of
water. Rarely have we had an
experience like it, and it
certainly is not good.

Video posted to Twitter following
Hurricane Florence, 19 September 2018

"

The Pledge of Allegiance to our great Country, in St. Louis Park, Minnesota, is under siege. That is why I am going to win the Great State of Minnesota in the 2020 Election. People are sick and tired of this stupidity and disloyalty to our wonderful USA!

"

Twitter, 11 July 2019

Let 'em leave. They're always telling us how to run it, how to do this, how to do that. You know what? If they don't love it, tell 'em to leave it.

Referencing Democratic congresswomen Ilhan Omar, Alexandria Ocasio-Cortez, Ayanna Pressley and Rashida Tlaib, 2020 campaign rally, 18 July 2019

66

They are trying to stop ME,
because I am fighting for YOU!

99

Twitter, 28 September 2019

66

As I learn more and more each
day, I am coming to the conclusion
that what is taking place is not
an impeachment, it is a COUP,
intended to take away the Power
of the People, their VOTE,
their Freedoms, their Second
Amendment, Religion, Military,
Border Wall, and their God-given
rights as a Citizen of The United
States of America!

99

Twitter, 2 October 2019

....

CHAPTER
THREE

ENEMIES

So [Barack Obama] could have come into the country, and they did it for social reasons... They did it for whatever reason... But he could have been born outside of this country. Why can't he produce a birth certificate and by the way, there is one story that his family doesn't even know what hospital he was born in!

Fox News, 28 March 2011

66

An 'extremely credible source'
has called my office and told
me that @BarackObama's birth
certificate is a fraud.

99

Twitter, 6 August 2012

66

My Twitter has become so powerful that I can actually make my enemies tell the truth. **99**

Twitter, 17 October 2012

66

I ask you to judge me by the enemies I have made. – Franklin D. Roosevelt.

99

Quoting a former president, Twitter, 21 November 2012

How amazing, the State Health Director who verified copies of Obama's 'birth certificate' died in plane crash today. All others lived.

Twitter, 12 December 2013

66

Rosie is crude, rude, obnoxious
and dumb – other than that I like
her very much!

99

*On his arch-nemesis, actress
Rosie O'Donnell, Twitter, 11 July 2014*

66

Donald J. Trump is calling for a complete and total shutdown of Muslims entering the United States until our country's representatives can figure out what the hell is going on.

99

Charleston rally following the
San Bernardino shooting, 7 December 2015

Iran is a very big problem and will continue to be. But if I'm not elected President, I know how to deal with trouble. And believe me, that's why I'm going to be elected President, folks.

Address to the American Israel Public Affairs Committee, 21 March 2016

66

Lyin' Ted Cruz just used a picture of Melania from a GQ shoot in his ad. Be careful, Lyin' Ted, or I will spill the beans on your wife!

99

Twitter, 23 March 2016

66

I started talking about the World Trade Center and the incredible bravery of everybody, of the police, our firemen, our everybody... and I've got this guy standing over there, looking at me, talking about New York values, with scorn on his face, with hatred of New York.

99

On his presidential rival Ted Cruz at a New York rally, 7 April 2016

66

The only card [Hillary Clinton] has is the woman's card. She's got nothing else to offer and frankly, if Hillary Clinton were a man, I don't think she'd get 5 per cent of the vote. The only thing she's got going is the woman's card, and the beautiful thing is, women don't like her.

99

Q&A with journalists, 26 April 2016

"

When Mexico sends its people,
they're not sending the best.
They're sending people that
have lots of problems and they're
bringing those problems.
They're bringing drugs, they're
bringing crime. They're rapists
and some, I assume, are good
people, but I speak to border
guards and they're telling us
what we're getting.

"

Candidacy announcement speech,
16 June 2016

"

Happy New Year to all, including to my many enemies and those who have fought me and lost so badly they just don't know what to do. Love!

"

Twitter, 31 December 2016

"

Any negative polls are fake news, just like the CNN, ABC, NBC polls in the election.

"

Twitter, 6 February 2017

"

The FAKE NEWS media (failing @nytimes, @CNN, @NBCNews and many more) is not my enemy, it is the enemy of the American people. SICK!

"

Twitter, 17 February 2017

66

You are witnessing the single greatest WITCH HUNT in American political history – led by some very bad and conflicted people. **99**

On the story that there was collusion with Russia, Twitter, 15 June 2017

"

Being nice to Rocket Man
hasn't worked in 25 years, why
would it work now? Clinton failed,
Bush failed, and Obama failed.
I won't fail.

"

Twitter, 1 October 2017

66

The media is – really, the word,
I think one of the greatest of all
terms I've come up with – is fake.
I guess other people have used it,
perhaps over the years, but I've
never noticed it.

99

Trinity Broadcasting Network,
26 October 2017

"

WITCH HUNT!

"

Twitter, 27 February 2018

The new Fake News narrative is that there is CHAOS in the White House. Wrong! People will always come & go, and I want strong dialogue before making a final decision. I still have some people that I want to change (always seeking perfection). There is no Chaos, only great Energy!

Twitter, 6 March 2018

"

The Washington Post said I refer to Jeff Sessions as 'Mr. Magoo' and Rod Rosenstein as 'Mr. Peepers.' This is 'according to people with whom the president has spoken.' There are no such people and don't know these characters... just more Fake & Disgusting News to create ill will!

"

Twitter, 21 April 2018

"

Congratulations America, we are now into the second year of the greatest Witch Hunt in American History... and there is still No Collusion and No Obstruction. The only Collusion was that done by Democrats who were unable to win an Election despite the spending of far more money!

"

Twitter, 17 May 2018

66

Wow, just learned in the Failing
New York Times that the corrupt
former leaders of the FBI, almost
all fired or forced to leave the
agency for some very bad reasons,
opened up an investigation on me,
for no reason & with no proof,
after I fired Lyin' James Comey,
a total sleaze!

99

Twitter, 12 January 2019

66

...The good news is that we are winning. Our real opponent is not the Democrats, or the dwindling number of Republicans that lost their way and got left behind, our primary opponent is the Fake News Media. In the history of our Country, they have never been so bad!

99

Twitter, 2 September 2019

66

Rep. Adam Schiff totally made up my conversation with Ukraine President and read it to Congress and Millions. He must resign and be investigated. He has been doing this for two years. He is a sick man!

99

Twitter, 27 September 2019

66

The Do Nothing Democrats should be focused on building up our Country, not wasting everyone's time and energy on BULLSHIT, which is what they have been doing ever since I got overwhelmingly elected in 2016, 223–306. Get a better candidate this time, you'll need it!

99

Creating problems for broadcasters' policies around expletives, Twitter, 2 October 2019

....

CHAPTER
FOUR

DIPLOMACY

"

I have to start by saying I'm a big fan, a very big fan, of the United Nations and all it stands for... the concept of the United Nations and the fact that the United Nations is in New York is very important to me and very important to the world, as far as I am concerned. So I am a big fan.

"

Senate committee hearing on renovation of UN headquarters, 21 July 2005

66

The concept of global warming
was created by and for the Chinese
in order to make US manufacturing
non-competitive.

99

Twitter, 6 November 2012

66

What will we get for bombing Syria besides more debt and a possible long-term conflict? Obama needs Congressional approval.

99

Twitter, 29 August 2013

AGAIN, TO OUR VERY
FOOLISH LEADER, DO NOT
ATTACK SYRIA – IF YOU DO,
VERY MANY BAD THINGS WILL
HAPPEN & FROM THAT FIGHT
THE US GETS NOTHING.

Twitter, 5 September 2013

If the morons who killed all of those people at Charlie Hebdo would have just waited, the magazine would have folded – no money, no success!

Twitter, 14 January 2014

I believe Putin will continue to re-build the Russian Empire. He has zero respect for Obama or the US!

Twitter, 22 March 2014

66

Putin has shown the world
what happens when America
has weak leaders. Peace
Through Strength!

Twitter, 28 April 2014

66

I own Miss Universe, I was in
Russia, I was in Moscow recently
and I spoke, indirectly and directly,
with President Putin, who could
not have been nicer, and we had
a tremendous success.

99

National Press Club speech,
27 May 2014

66

By the way, I have great respect for China. I have many Chinese friends. They live in my buildings all over the place.

99

National Press Club speech,
27 May 2014

I beat the people from China. I win against China. You can win against China if you're smart. But our people don't have a clue. We give state dinners to the heads of China. I said, 'Why are you doing state dinners for them? They're ripping us left and right. Just take them to McDonald's and go back to the negotiating table.'

Campaign event, 21 July 2015

When I become President, the days of treating Israel like a second-class citizen will end on day one.

Address to the American Israel Public Affairs Committee, 21 March 2016

We will move the American
embassy to the eternal capital of
the Jewish people, Jerusalem.

*Address to the American Israel Public
Affairs Committee, 21 March 2016*

"

If Russia or any other country
or person has Hillary Clinton's
33,000 illegally deleted emails,
perhaps they should share them
with the FBI!

"

Twitter, 27 July 2016

" Russia will have much greater respect for our country when I am leading it than when other people have led it. **"**

CNN, 11 January 2017

"

You have a bunch of bad hombres down there. You aren't doing enough to stop them. I think your military is scared. Our military isn't, so I might just send them down to take care of it.

"

Phone call to Mexican President Enrique Pena Nieto, January 2017

"

And I can tell you, speaking for
myself, I own nothing in Russia.
I have no loans in Russia. I don't
have any deals in Russia. President
Putin called me up very nicely to
congratulate me on the win of
the election.

"

News conference, 16 February 2017

66

You know, you're in such great shape... beautiful.

99

Caught on camera speaking to Brigitte Macron, wife of French leader Emmanuel Macron, 13 July 2017

"

The people of this country should be very comfortable, and I will tell you this: If North Korea does anything in terms of even thinking about (attacking) anybody that we love or we represent or our allies or us, they can be very, very nervous.

"

Press conference, 10 August 2017

66

No, I want to thank [Vladimir Putin], because we're trying to cut down on payroll. And as far as I'm concerned, I'm very thankful that he let go of a large number of people because now we have a smaller payroll.

99

Referring to Vladimir Putin's expulsion of US diplomats, press conference, 10 August 2017

"

There's no – there is no collusion.
You know why? Because I don't
speak to Russians. **"**

Press conference, 10 August 2017

Why would Kim Jong-un insult me by calling me 'old', when I would NEVER call him 'short and fat'? Oh well, I try so hard to be his friend – and maybe some day that will happen!

Twitter, 12 November 2017

66

The UN is not a friend of democracy, it's not a friend to freedom, it's not a friend even to the United States… and it surely is not a friend to Israel… I will veto any attempt by the UN to impose its will on the Jewish state.

99

Twitter, 23 December 2017

"

North Korean Leader Kim Jong-Un just stated that the 'Nuclear Button is on his desk at all times.' Will someone from his depleted and food-starved regime please inform him that I too have a Nuclear Button, but it is a much bigger & more powerful one than his, and my Button works!

"

Twitter, 3 January 2018

66

My fellow Americans – a short time ago, I ordered the United States armed forces to launch precision strikes on targets associated with the chemical weapons capabilities of Syrian dictator Bashar al-Assad. A combined operation with the armed forces of France and the United Kingdom is now under way. We thank them both.

99

Televised address to the nation,
13 April 2018

"

To Iran and to Russia, I ask:
what kind of nation wants to be
associated with the mass murder
of innocent men, women and
children? The nations of the world
can be judged by the friends they
keep. No nation can succeed
in the long run by promoting
rogue states, brutal tyrants, and
murderous dictators.

"

Televised address to the nation,
13 April 2018

I actually told Theresa May how to do it but she didn't agree, she didn't listen to me. She wanted to go a different route. I would actually say that she probably went the opposite way. And that is fine. She should negotiate the best way she knows how. But it is too bad what is going on.

On Britain's Brexit negotiations,
The Sun, *13 July 2018*

"

To Iranian President Rouhani:
NEVER, EVER THREATEN THE
UNITED STATES AGAIN OR YOU
WILL SUFFER CONSEQUENCES
THE LIKES OF WHICH FEW
THROUGHOUT HISTORY HAVE
EVER SUFFERED BEFORE. WE
ARE NO LONGER A COUNTRY
THAT WILL STAND FOR
YOUR DEMENTED WORDS
OF VIOLENCE & DEATH.
BE CAUTIOUS!

"

Twitter, 23 July 2018

"

No Collusion, No Obstruction,
Complete and Total
EXONERATION. KEEP
AMERICA GREAT!

"

In response to Robert Mueller's
report on Russian interference in the
2016 election, 24 March 2019

"

@SadiqKhan, who by all accounts has done a terrible job as Mayor of London, has been foolishly 'nasty' to the visiting President of the United States, by far the most important ally of the United Kingdom. He is a stone-cold loser who should focus on crime in London, not me...

...Kahn reminds me very much of our very dumb and incompetent Mayor of NYC, de Blasio, who has also done a terrible job – only half his height. In any event, I look forward to being a great friend to the United Kingdom, and am looking very much forward to my visit. Landing now!

"

Twitter, 3 June 2019

66

The meeting with the queen was incredible... we had automatic chemistry, you understand that feeling, it's a good feeling... I had a great relationship... There are those that say they have never seen the queen have a better time, a more animated time. We had a period where we were talking solid straight. I didn't even know who the other people at the table were; I never spoke to them.

99

On meeting Queen Elizabeth II,
Fox News, 6 June 2019

"

LONDON needs a new mayor ASAP. Khan is a disaster – will only get worse!

Twitter, 15 June 2019

66

China gets 91% of its Oil from the Straight [sic], Japan 62%, & many other countries likewise. So why are we protecting the shipping lanes for other countries (many years) for zero compensation. All of these countries should be protecting their own ships on what has always been a dangerous journey. We don't even need to be there in that the U.S. has just become (by far) the largest producer of Energy anywhere in the world!

99

Twitter, 24 June 2019

> Iran leadership doesn't understand the words 'nice' or 'compassion,' they never have. Sadly, the thing they do understand is Strength and Power, and the USA is by far the most powerful Military Force in the world... Any attack by Iran on anything American will be met with great and overwhelming force. In some areas, overwhelming will mean obliteration. No more John Kerry & Obama!

Twitter, 25 June 2019

66

Leaving South Korea after a wonderful meeting with Chairman Kim Jong-Un. Stood on the soil of North Korea, an important statement for all, and a great honor!

99

Twitter, 30 June 2019

We have a really good man who's going to be the prime minister of the UK now. He's tough and he's smart. They're saying, 'Britain Trump'. They call him 'Britain Trump' and people are saying that's a good thing… They like me over there. That's what they wanted. That's what they need. He'll get it done. Boris is good. He's gonna do a good job.

Washington speech, 23 July 2019

66

France just put a digital tax on
our great American technology
companies. If anybody taxes them,
it should be their home Country,
the USA. We will announce a
substantial reciprocal action on
Macron's foolishness shortly. I've
always said American wine is
better than French wine!

99

Twitter, 26 July 2019

We are winning, and we will win. They should not have broken the deal we had with them. Happy Birthday China!

Twitter, 30 September 2019

CHAPTER
FIVE

INSULTS

"

Do you mind if I sit back a little bit? Because your breath is very bad. It really is. Has this ever been told to you before?

"

Larry King Live, 15 April 1989

"

I really understand beauty. And I will tell you, [Angeline Jolie's] not – I do own Miss Universe. I do own Miss USA. I mean I own a lot of different things. I do understand beauty, and she's not.

"

Larry King Live, CNN, October 2007

66

@ariannahuff is unattractive
both inside and out. I fully
understand why her former
husband left her for a man –
he made a good decision.

99

Twitter, 28 August 2012

Robert Pattinson should not take back Kristen Stewart. She cheated on him like a dog & will do it again – just watch. He can do much better!

Twitter, 17 October 2012

66

While @BetteMidler is an
extremely unattractive woman,
I refuse to say that because I
always insist on being
politically correct.

99

Twitter, 28 October 2012

"

Is PM Cameron a dummy? With monumental cuts in UK spending, how come he continues to spend billions of pounds...

"

Twitter, 6 December 2012

66

@Lord_Sugar – unlike you, I own
The Apprentice. You were never
successful enough, but I approved
you anyway. Without my show,
you'd be nothing!

99

Twitter, 6 December 2012

Sorry losers and haters, but my IQ is one of the highest – and you all know it! Please don't feel so stupid or insecure, it's not your fault.

Twitter, 8 May 2013

"

Just tried watching *Modern Family* – written by a moron, really boring. Writer has the mind of a very dumb and backward child. Sorry Danny!

"

Twitter, 13 June 2013

Sadly, because President Obama has done such a poor job as president, you won't see another black president for generations! 🙷🙷

Twitter, 25 November 2014

66

If Hillary Clinton can't satisfy her
husband, what makes her think
she can satisfy America?

99

Deleted tweet, Twitter, 16 April 2015

Marco Rubio was a complete
disaster today in an interview
with Chris Wallace @FoxNews
concerning our invading Iraq.
He was as clueless as Jeb.

Twitter, 18 May 2015

66

Jeb Bush gave five different answers in four days on whether or not we should have invaded Iraq. He is so confused. Not presidential material!

99

Twitter, 18 May 2015

> **"** He's not a war hero. He was a war hero because he was captured. I like people who weren't captured. **"**

Speaking of John McCain, who spent five and a half years as a prisoner of war in Vietnam, 18 July 2015

66

How can a dummy dope like Harry Hurt, who wrote a failed book about me but doesn't know me or anything about me, be on TV discussing Trump?

99

Twitter, 29 July 2015

"

She gets out and she starts asking me all sorts of ridiculous questions. There was blood coming out of her eyes, blood coming out of her wherever…

"

On facing tough questioning from Fox News' Megyn Kelly, CNN, 7 August 2015

66

Sadly, she's no longer a 10.

99

On Heidi Klum, 15 August 2015

Huma Abedin, the top aide to Hillary Clinton and the wife of perv sleazebag Anthony Wiener, was a major security risk as a collector of info.

Twitter, 31 August 2015

"

Look at that face! Would anyone vote for that? Can you imagine that, the face of our next president?!

"

Commenting on Republican candidate Carly Fiorina, Rolling Stone, *September 2015*

"

Jeb said, 'we were safe with my brother. We were safe.' Well, the World Trade Center just fell down! Now, am I trying to blame him? I'm not blaming anybody. But the World Trade Center came down. So when he said, 'we were safe', that's not safe.

"

Fox News Sunday, 18 October 2015

"

Meryl Streep, one of the most over-rated actresses in Hollywood, doesn't know me but attacked last night at the Golden Globes. She is a Hillary flunky who lost big.

"

Twitter, 9 January 2017

"

I heard poorly rated @Morning_ Joe speaks badly of me (don't watch anymore). Then how come low I.Q. Crazy Mika, along with Psycho Joe, came to Mar-a-Lago 3 nights in a row around New Year's Eve, and insisted on joining me. She was bleeding badly from a face-lift. I said no!

"

Twitter, 29 June 2017

Crooked Hillary is the worst (and biggest) loser of all time. She just can't stop... Hillary, get on with your life and give it another try in three years!

Twitter, 18 November 2017

> Crazy Joe Biden is trying to act like a tough guy. Actually, he is weak, both mentally and physically, and yet he threatens me, for the second time, with physical assault. He doesn't know me, but he would go down fast and hard, crying all the way. Don't threaten people Joe!

Twitter, 22 March 2018

66

Robert De Niro, a very Low IQ
individual, has received too many
shots to the head by real boxers
in movies. I watched him last
night and truly believe he may be
'punch-drunk.' I guess he doesn't
realize the economy is the best
it's ever been with employment
being at an all-time high, and many
companies pouring back into our
country. Wake up Punchy!

99

Twitter, 13 June 2018

> "Congresswoman Maxine Waters, an extraordinarily low IQ person, has become, together with Nancy Pelosi, the Face of the Democrat Party. She has just called for harm to supporters, of which there are many, of the Make America Great Again movement. Be careful what you wish for Max!"

Twitter, 25 June 2018

"

Mike Pompeo is doing a great job, I am very proud of him. His predecessor, Rex Tillerson, didn't have the mental capacity needed. He was dumb as a rock and I couldn't get rid of him fast enough. He was lazy as hell. Now it is a whole new ballgame, great spirit at State!

"

Twitter, 7 December 2018

66

So it was indeed (just proven in court papers) 'last in his class' (Annapolis) John McCain that sent the Fake Dossier to the FBI and Media hoping to have it printed BEFORE the Election. He & the Dems, working together, failed (as usual). Even the Fake News refused this garbage!

99

Twitter, 17 March 2019

CHAPTER
SIX

TOP
TRUMPS

"

The person who came up with
the expression 'the weaker sex'
was either very naive or had to
be kidding. I have seen women
manipulate men with just a twitch
of their eye – or perhaps another
body part.

"

Trump: The Art of the Comeback, *1997*

"

I love women. They've come into my life. They've gone out of my life. Even those who have exited somewhat ungracefully still have a place in my heart. I only have one regret in the women department – that I never had the opportunity to court Lady Diana Spencer. I met her on a number of occasions.

"

Trump: The Art of the Comeback, *1997*

"
All of the women on *The Apprentice* flirted with me – consciously or unconsciously. That's to be expected.

How to Get Rich, *2004*

❝

Before a show, I'll go backstage and everyone's getting dressed, and everything else, and you know, no men are anywhere, and I'm allowed to go in because I'm the owner of the pageant and therefore I'm inspecting it... You know, they're standing there with no clothes. And you see these incredible looking women, and so, I sort of get away with things like that. **❞**

Speaking about the Miss America pageant, 2005

"
You know, I'm automatically attracted to beautiful – I just start kissing them. It's like a magnet. Just kiss. I don't even wait. And when you're a star, they let you do it. You can do anything.... Grab them by the pussy. You can do anything.

"

Speaking to Billy Bush on the Access Hollywood *tape, 2005*

I don't think Ivanka would do that inside the magazine. Although she does have a very nice figure. I've said that if Ivanka weren't my daughter, perhaps I would be dating her.

Responding to a question about how he would feel if Ivanka posed for Playboy, The View, 2006

66

The worst things in history have happened when people stop thinking for themselves and listen to other people and, even worse, start following other people. That's what gives rise to dictators. **99**

Think Like a Champion, *2009*

❝

It's like in golf. A lot of people – I don't want this to sound trivial – but a lot of people are switching to these really long putters, very unattractive. It's weird. You see these great players with these really long putters, because they can't sink three-footers anymore. And, I hate it. I am a traditionalist. I have so many fabulous friends who happen to be gay, but I am a traditionalist.

❞

Sharing his thoughts on gay marriage,
New York Times, *11 May 2011*

66

But I don't know why Obama gets credit for the whole bin Laden thing. He's sitting there. He's got three choices, leave him alone – which nobody would do – take him out with a missile, or take him out with the military. So he said, 'Take him out with the military.' OK. Congratulations.

99

CNN, 8 December 2011

66

I have a great relationship with the blacks. I've always had a great relationship with the blacks.

99

Talk1300 in Albany, 11 April 2012

66

I have never seen a thin person
drinking Diet Coke.

99

Twitter, 14 October 2012

66

Who wouldn't take Kate's picture and make lots of money if she does the nude sunbathing thing. Come on Kate!

99

On Kate Middleton, Twitter,
17 September 2012

66
Leadership: Whatever happens, you're responsible. If it doesn't happen, you're responsible.

99

Twitter, 8 November 2013

66

Windmills are the greatest threat in the US to both bald and golden eagles. Media claims fictional 'global warming' is worse.

99

Twitter, 9 September 2014

I think apologizing's a great thing, but you have to be wrong. I will absolutely apologize, sometime in the hopefully distant future, if I'm ever wrong.

The Tonight Show, *11 September 2015*

"

I am totally in favour of vaccines. But I want smaller doses over a longer period of time. Same exact amount, but you take this little beautiful baby, and you pump – I mean, it looks just like it's meant for a horse, not for a child, and we've had so many instances, people that work for me. … [in which] a child, a beautiful child went to have the vaccine, and came back and a week later had a tremendous fever, got very, very sick, now is autistic.

"

CNN presidential debate, September 2015

It's really cold outside, they are calling it a major freeze, weeks ahead of normal. Man, we could use a big fat dose of global warming!

Twitter, 19 October 2015

66

His wife, if you look at his wife, she was standing there. She had nothing to say. She probably ... maybe she wasn't allowed to have anything to say. You tell me. But plenty of people have written that. She was extremely quiet. And it looked like she had nothing to say.

99

Referring to Ghazala Khan, mother of a fallen Muslim soldier, ABC, July 2016

If she gets to pick her judges
– nothing you can do, folks.
Although, the Second
Amendment people. Maybe
there is. I don't know.

Referring to Hillary Clinton,
campaign rally, 9 August 2016

66

I have tremendous respect for women and the many roles they serve that are vital to the fabric of our society and our economy. **99**

Twitter, 8 March 2017

❝

Despite the constant negative
press covfefe…

❞

*The tweet that sent the internet into
a frenzy as people tried to work out what
"covfefe" meant, 31 May 2017*

"

You know, I go to Washington and I see all these politicians, and I see the swamp. And it's not a good place. In fact, today I said we ought to change it from the word 'swamp' to the word 'cesspool' or, perhaps, to the word 'sewer'.

"

National Scout Jamboree,
24 July 2017

66

What you're seeing and what you're reading is not what's happening.

*Veterans Association speech,
25 July 2018*

66

It is a very scary time for young men in America, where you can be guilty of something you may not be guilty of… Women are doing great.

99

Reflecting on the #MeToo movement, October 2018

"

The Fake News is not as important,
or as powerful, as Social Media...
When I ultimately leave office
in six years, or maybe 10 or 14
(just kidding), they will quickly
go out of business for lack of
credibility... That's why they will all
be Endorsing me at some point,
one way or the other. Could you
imagine having Sleepy Joe Biden,
or Alfred E. Newman or a very

nervous and skinny version of Pocahontas (1/1024th), as your President, rather than what you have now, so great looking and smart, a true Stable Genius! Sorry to say that even Social Media would be driven out of business along with, and finally, the Fake News Media!

99

Twitter, 11 July 2019

"

In the beautiful Midwest, windchill temperatures are reaching minus 60 degrees, the coldest ever recorded. In coming days, expected to get even colder. People can't last outside even for minutes. What the hell is going on with Global Warming? Please come back fast, we need you! **"**

Twitter, 29 January 2019